Kennebunkport Recollections

Written by Grace H Brock

Compiled by Christine Rigden

Chris

Lle Noddfa Books

Bedworth, England

First published in Great Britain in 2012

Lle Noddfa Books
Bedworth, Warwickwhire.

Copyright © 2012 Lle Noddfa Books.
All rights reserved.

ISBN 978 0 951 3221 2 5

Editing and Typesetting by Christine Rigden
Front cover illustration by Christine Rigden
Printing by Lulu.com

Articles written by Grace Hanson Brock,
probably between 1960 and 1972.

This collection compiled by Christine Rigden in 2012.

Background information from her daughters
Priscilla Brock Baker
and Celia Brock Conrad

Contents

Introduction	- 3 -
Growing up	- 5 -
The River	- 9 -
The River Carnival	- 11 -
The Summer People	- 15 -
Cemetery Hill	- 21 -
Goodwin's	- 23 -
Winter	- 27 -
Pungin'	- 31 -
The Day I Quit Writing for Good	- 35 -
The Olympian Club	- 37 -
Riding the Electrics	- 41 -
Barkers Ridge	- 45 -
The Street Where I Live	- 53 -
Snow on Broad Street	- 55 -
Progress	- 57 -
About Grace Brock	- 59 -

Kennebunkport Recollections

Introduction

Seventy today is a wonderful age, for you have seen this whole modern age develop. When I was a little child in Kennebunkport, Maine, we had neither electricity nor indoor plumbing, though they were common in the larger cities.

Along the river banks, shipyards were still building fishing schooners, and many of the old clipper ship captains were still alive. It used to seem to me that it must be pretty dull for them, just puttering around their yards down by the river, smoking their pipes, when they had once sailed their ships around the world, from Boston to Bangkok, from Salem to Shanghai.

Along the river banks where the gift shops and the art studios now flourish there were once shipyards where fishing schooners were built. On Saturdays in spring we children would play there all day, climbing around and among the timbers and enjoying the mingled smells of salt air and new lumber.

There were lots of things for a child to do in Kennebunkport. As soon as it was warm enough to wear sneakers, we were off to the high rocky cliffs that bordered the shore. There we would race up and down the cliffs where a miss-step would mean certain death, as sure-footed as young goats. But I never knew a child to come to harm.

Grace Hanson Brock
(Rochester, NH)

Kennebunkport Recollections

Growing up

I am a lucky person, for I grew up in Kennebunkport, Maine at the turn of the century, before the leveling conditions of modern life had brought about a dreary sameness among people everywhere. In those days rich people *looked* rich! They wore silk – silk sweaters, silk skirts, silk blouses and silk stockings. Today, we all look alike. That woman you see over there in the wildly patterned shift could be the wife of an important executive but she might just as well be a mill worker on vacation.

Probably this is a good thing, but it does make for a certain drabness. Even without the silks, in those days you could still tell the rich by speech and manners. The leveling influence of the mass media has made correct speech seem stuffy and good manners have become "putting on airs." We've all got to be "casual".

Today, with the huge cars crowding the roads, a Cadillac may hold a tycoon, a movie star, a bus driver or a gangster, but you are more likely to find the rich man in a small car. A big car is no longer a status symbol.

In the old days it was a thrill to a small native to see the rich ride out in their shining patent leather carriages, drawn by glittering horses with docked tails, and driven by liveried coachmen. Sometimes there would even be a footman! The women riding in the handsome victorias[1] and landaus[2] would be dressed in silk, naturally, and

---

[1] The victoria – an elegant French carriage; essentially a phaeton with the addition of a coachman's box-seat, and drawn by one or two horses.

[2] Landau – Another type of four-wheeled convertible carriage, usually

would be holding small silk parasols to shield their complexions. No leathery sunbaked skins for them!

At the turn of the century the Summer People, as we natives called them, came to the big houses along the cliffs in late June and stayed right through until Labor Day. Weeks before their arrival, the townspeople would be busy cleaning and repairing the big houses in the summer colony. As the day of their occupants' arrival drew closer the servants appeared, to make sure everything was in readiness. Servants – that was something! Usually they were colored, and a strange sight indeed in a Maine village. The then trunks would begin to arrive. Great horse-drawn drays piled high with trunks crawled slowly along Ocean Avenue, bound for the big hotels as well as the cottages. Even the hotel-dwellers stayed all summer.

Now, the Square became full of the Summer People. We gazed with awe at the children, accompanied by their nurses or governesses. That was one good thing about not being rich – you didn't always have to have a grownup tagging along!

And then there was the river! It fairly swarmed with canoes of all colors, decorated with gold stripes, silver stripes, all kinds of stripes. Most family canoes had names carefully inscribed on the bows. There were very few motor boats, just enough to rock the canoes pleasantly as they went chugging by.

We children partially lived in or on the river. Sometimes we would paddle far up above the landing

---

drawn by two or four horses

where the tide no longer reached, where cranes stood in the reeds along the banks and squirrels chattered in the tall trees above. We often took our lunches and stayed all day; but we had to be careful not to stay too long, or the tide would go out and leave us stranded on the mudflats.

We knew every inch of the river, just how to get up through the locks at half tide, and just how to shoot the small rapids by the Golf Club when the tide was low.

Sometimes we took our lunches to the beach instead, but no-one drove us. Grownups didn't consider themselves responsible for their children's entertainment as they do today, and if we wanted to go anywhere we walked or rode our bicycles. Our parents never seemed to worry about us, and why should they? There was nothing and no-one to harm us – no wildly racing cars, or strange perverted people around them.

In August came the highlight of the summer, the races at Picnic Rock. Down river was a long, straight stretch of water which afforded the hundreds of people seated on the banks an unobstructed view of the whole course. There were all kinds of races – men's and women's singles and doubles, men's war canoes and rowboats. Best of all, sometimes a few of the Penobscot Indians, who camped in the summer at the foot of the river, would show us what paddling *really* was. Tall, dark and silent, they would glide over the water, their paddles making hardly a sound but moving with awesome speed. We couldn't get over it!

Kennebunkport Recollections

The River

The Kennebunk! I would like to paraphrase Daniel Webster's famous words about Dartmouth College – a small river, but there are those who love it! I suspect that it no longer fills such an important place in the lives of the populace as it did in my youth and long before, for the Kennebunk has been a useful river. In the great days of the sailing vessels, many fine ships were built at the Landing and floated down the river to the sea.

Just below the Golf Club there were locks to hold the water back, but even in my day only a few great granite blocks on each side of the river remained. Fishing schooners were still being built in several shipyards along the banks, then. I remember one in particular, just behind the Congregational Church, where we children used to play when the workmen had gone. I can still smell the bayberry, the wild roses, the cool salt air and the new lumber.

As soon as we children learned to swim, we spent most of our time either in or on the river. There were plenty of canoes at our disposal, and when the tide was right we spent whole days exploring it. Sometimes we'd paddle all the way up through the Landing Bridge to the end of the tidewater and beyond. Gliding silently along, we often surprised a tall blue heron, standing solemnly on one leg, as he watched for unwary fish, while squirrels chattered in the trees above our heads.

There were many little creeks branching off the main river, and these made fine swimming places, if you could keep from touching bottom. Mud and eelgrass made that unpleasant. Firebrand Creek was a favorite place for picnics, especially at sunset when the water reflected the rosy light from the sky.

Sometimes we would land at Picnic Rock, where a high ledge rose high above the water, and its wooded sides were crisscrossed with little paths where we loved to run.

Today, the river is as beautiful as ever, but I miss the bright-colored canoes which used to dot its surface on sunny summer afternoons. There were hundreds of them in those days, painted every color imaginable – blue and green, red and white, yellow and purple, each gaily striped with its name painted on bow and stern. Almost everyone owned a canoe, or hired one. For many years Indians camped at the mouth of the river, and rented them to people who stayed at the hotels. They acted as guides, too, and we children watched with awe at their silent skill. People used to like to sit on the piazza of Goodwin's Ice Cream Parlor, which was built out over the water near the drawbridge on Dock Square, to watch the bright canoes go by.

Somehow in my mind I always see the river at full tide, mirror-like, reflecting its bands and taking its color from a sky of cloudless blue, though I know full well it can be otherwise on a grey day when the tide is out.

Perhaps the Kennebunk was loveliest in the fall, when the sky and the water were a deeper blue, and the maples blazed red and gold against the dark evergreens along its banks. But any time of year I loved it, and still do.

The River Carnival

It's Carnival night in Kennebunkport fifty years ago! All day people had been pouring into town in every conceivable kind of conveyance. They have come by trolley, horse and buggy, by farm wagon and hayrack and even, in a very few cases, by automobile. These last were followed everywhere by curious glances for, with their long linen dusters and goggles, their Dutch-looking caps and huge hats tied on with chiffon veils, they looked like creatures from another world, as indeed they were – the world of today!

When I was a girl, fifty years or so ago, it was my delight to paddle down the river about sunset to watch the last-minute preparations for the great event. All along the shore people would be stringing Japanese lanterns along each private wharf and riverside cottage, and each raft would have its complement of eager workers adding the final touches to their entries. The far shore of the river had no docks or houses but was a steep rocky bank covered with fir trees. The land belonged to Mr Rogers, and each year his men outlined the shore with red paper lanterns on bamboo poles a few feet apart. When they were lighted they blossomed softly against the dark shore. A lovely sight!

By this time the other bank of the river, where the board-walk ran from the village down to the sea, would be black with people who had come early so as to get the best possible vantage point from which to watch the gorgeous spectacle. At the foot of the river was the Boat Club, and there was a scene of furious activity for you, for it was there that the most elaborate floats gathered, ready to head the procession up-river. Of course at the last moment some vitally important detail would be discovered to be missing, or some particularly lovely lantern would be drooped in the water or set afire by the hasty fingers trying to light it.

We had some pretty impressive floats in those days, I can tell you! Once an ambitious group constructed a replica of the Statue of Liberty with May Atkins, our pretty blond music teacher, posing as the goddess. She stood motionless, holding her torch aloft all the way up the river and back! We couldn't see how she did it.

Soon it was time to hurry back upriver to help paddle our family canoe, which was usually fastened to that of a neighbor, catamaran-style. A bamboo framework was then constructed and hung with dozens of lanterns. It was a tricky thing to manage, loaded as it was with six people, including a small and active boy. Then, too, we had to paddle against the tide if we were to join the other canoes in the glittering parade up the river.

When it became dark, every wharf and house along the shore gleamed softly, outlined with many-colored lanterns. We usually drew up against the banks little above the Boat Club, to watch the procession as it formed behind the band, which was seated on a large raft drawn slowly along by a powerful motor boat.

No-one who has not seen it can imagine the magical sight of hundreds of canoes and floats all hung with Japanese lanterns, filling the river from shore to shore as they glided silently along, their beauty doubled by the shimmering reflections in the dark water.

At last they reached the drawbridge which had been opened for the occasion, and swept through to turn in a glittering circle in the wide basin above the bridge amid the cheers and applause of the admiring throng. Then the tide turned back toward the sea and the procession with its softly gleaming lights and music followed, gliding slowly back to the Club House.

Now the fireworks, which had been set up at the Rogers boathouse across the river from the Boat Club, began to go off, showering gold and green, crimson, blue and white stars against the dark sky. There were Roman candles and rockets, pinwheels and fountains, and occasional set pieces which never failed to draw cries of admiration and loud bursts of applause from the spectators.

There was occasional excitement in the canoes now as candles burned low, and here and there a lantern caught fire. But it was a simple matter to douse the flame in the river with no harm done.

At last the final set piece, the American Flag, was set off as the band played the Star Spangled Banner, and the Carnival was over. The lanterns in the canoes and along the shore were put out, one by one, and the canoes drifted homeward. Now all were gone, and the river lay dark and silent beneath the stars.

The Summer People

We were glad to see them come and glad to see them go, as I've heard grandparents say of visiting grandchildren. We used to get pretty sick of them before they finally left, the day before Labor Day; but in April, after a long hard winter and the ordeal of mud-time, it was the most exciting thing in the world to watch the preparations for their arrival.

First, sometimes even before the snow was gone, all the available men and women in our village would head for the shore where the big hotels and cottages were. The men would take down shutters, repair damage done by winter storms and spruce up the grounds, while the women cleaned like crazy.

The minute school was out we children would mount our bikes, if we had any, and race down Ocean Avenue to watch the workmen and, if we were lucky, earn a nickel or so running errands. When the season was well advanced, cutting grass or weeding gardens might pay as much as a dime. At that time it was a lot of money!

At last June would come and all was ready. The first to arrive would be the servants, very proud and haughty in their crisp uniforms and very critical of the work the villagers had done. Then heavy drays[3] piled high with trunks would begin to appear on Ocean Avenue, for in the early 1900s (the time of which I write) people didn't flit from place to place all summer as they do now. They

---

[3] Dray – a low, flat cart used for haulage

came with their children, servants, pets, and goodness knows what all, and stayed.

Day after day Pullman cars, names lettered in gold on their glittering sides, would pull into our little branch station direct from Boston, New York, Philadelphia, Montreal, or even Chicago! It was hard for us to imagine travelling such distances, for most of us had hardly been out of our own village. Often the Summer People arrived in private cars. Think of having a whole car to yourself!

No child would miss seeing these great trains pull in. First, there'd be a far-away shriek of the train whistle, which was a signal for the liveried coachmen waiting in the handsome carriages behind the station to descend from their lofty seats and proceed to the station platform to greet their employers and carry their luggage. To us children, our hearts pounding with excitement, the tension almost unbearable. But just in time to save us, with one last shriek, the train would whiz around the curve and, with a great hissing of brakes and a chuff-chuffing of steam, would come to a halt. The white-coated porters would place step-stools below the train steps, and then the big moment, the Summer People would emerge!

We knew most of the old families by sight and would whisper excitedly every time a familiar figure appeared. I suppose we felt much as a later generation did, when standing in front of a theater after a 'world premiere' to watch the movie stars come out.

When all the summer People had left the station, we'd mount our bicycles and if we had any money, which was seldom, we'd stop at Goodwin's for an ice cream. We didn't carry wallets with folding money in them, as so many children seem to do now.

In those days there was a 'great gulf fixed' between the Summer People and us natives. The Summer People were rich and they LOOKED rich! How different today! With everyone in ragged jeans and sweatshirts you can hardly tell male from female, let along rich from poor. Perhaps this is a good thing but it IS monotonous!

Well, anyway, as I was saying, when I was a child the rich looked rich. The women wore lots of silk… silk skirts, silk sweaters, silk stockings, and they wore big hats with chiffon scarves floating around them. The men were equally resplendent in spotless white ducks or creamy flannels, striped blazers and straw hats with fancy ribbon bands.

The Summer People not only looked rich, they lived rich. They never seemed to work, which seemed very strange to us. They played tennis and golf (which we never dreamed of doing) and the older women drove to the golf club to tea in the afternoon in their patent leather victorias with tiny parasols to protect them from the sun. Their horses' tails were usually docked which looked very stylish, but we thought it was mean. How could they switch away the flies, we said.

At first it was exciting to see the river full of canoes again, and at mail time I tell you Dock Square was something to see, with crowds of people and horse-drawn vehicles of all kinds. And if the trolley happened to pull in with its bell clanging, frightening the horses and making them rear and plunge, it was as much as your life was worth to cross the street!

By the middle of August, however, with our pockets comfortably full, we began to feel crowded. There were so many of them and they took up so much room, with their fancy carriages, pulled by prancing horses. Then too, there were tennis rackets, golf clubs, and goodness knows what all! Much as your life was worth, it was, to cross Dock Square on a summer afternoon. A few of them even had automobiles, and of course the horses were scared to death of the noisy, smelly things, and they'd rear and plunge to beat the band! I tell you, it was something to see, when a couple of spans of horses[4] disputed the right of way with a Pierce-Arrow!

At last, the day before Labor Day would arrive. From early morning until sundown, Ocean Avenue would be full of heavy drays 'pulled by slow horses' as Tennyson says, and piled high with trunks and boxes. In those days, whole families came and stayed all summer which required many types of sporting equipment, as well as the required clothing to play the games. Then too, there would be dress clothes for balls and dinners as well as clothes for every day.

Finally Labor Day came, and with that peace descended on our village. There was a lovely, relaxed feeling in the air. We all sort of expanded – took up all the space we wanted – and were individuals again, standing out, each important in his own place. We knew everyone, and everyone knew us. No longer were we a nameless group, known to the Summer People as "the natives". Now, we walked slowly, and stopped to speak with friends in a leisurely fashion.

---

[4] Span of horses – a matched pair

It was pleasant to stroll down to the foot of the river without being crowded off the boardwalk by careless people who didn't seem to see us. In the soft, golden sunlight of September, we could idle along, stopping now and then to lean on the railing edging the boardwalk to watch the fishing boats, sails gleaming white against the blue river, or to look down through the clear water at the crabs or small fish swimming below. We could wander about the grounds of the summer cottages, watching the workmen putting up shutters and making all secure for the winter gales ahead. At the foot of the river was a raft, where it was great fun to lie in the warm sunlight as the water breathed in and out, like some big, gentle animal, and the raft rose and fell with the breathing.

Along the cliffs now the wild rose haws[5] were red, and the spicy smell of the bayberry mingled with the salt air. The ocean was the soft, hazy blue that occurs in early September, and the gentle swell broke softly on the rocks. Blowing Cave and Spouting Rock didn't blow or spout much now; after all, they'd been entertaining people all summer and were also having a much needed rest.

It was fun too, to climb around on the rocks and investigate the pools left by the tide. Down on the beach the gulls seemed bolder, as if they too felt somehow freer, and the little sandpipers skittered gaily along, paying no attention to us. We'd paddle in the still-warm water. The beach was ours again too, so we would spend time building tall sand castles. Toward sunset, we would stroll slowly home, thinking about supper and

---

[5] Rose haws – rose hips, the seed pods of the wild rose

hoping that there would be hot biscuits and homemade jam.

Soon, school would begin and the village social life, forsaken in the frantic pace of summer, would begin again. But right now there was an interlude, a lazy, dream time, and we enjoyed it to the fullest.

Cemetery Hill

A short time ago I learned from an item in the *Star* that the village of Kennebunkport had taken over the care of the Tombs cemetery. I understand that this was necessary before vandals wrecked it completely. The fallen stones needed to be re-set and the broken ones repaired. I expect the grass will be clipped and barbered, and the whole place will be a credit to the community.

But I cannot help casting a nostalgic glance backward to the time when it was a charming, half-wild spot, a sort of Secret Garden, where fragrant valley lilies grew thickly in the un-mown grass, and thick ground-phlox spread unhindered. Hidden from the road by the rise of ground over the tomb, we children could play in complete seclusion, and we spent many happy hours there.

In the center of the cemetery was a ledge, that most delightful of play-places. It was full of little hollows and crevices which caught the rain, and birds came there to drink and bathe. Beside the ledge and shading it, stood a big old pine. One of its great branches overspread the ledge, and every year a pair of robins built a nest there. The branch was so low that we could easily peer into the nest and watch everything that went on, from the first beautiful blue egg to the flight of the last fledgling. We even helped the parent birds in their frenzied efforts to keep those gaping mouths filled, and then we watched them teach their young to fly.

When we tired of playing on the ledge we'd wander around, looking at the old tombstones and reading the inscriptions. One we liked was directly over the tomb, and was actually a big stone table. We liked to sit under it, and eat the cookies we usually brought along to tide us over until the next meal.

But our favorite was a long slab of stone, held on edge by wrought-iron standards, and divided into three parts by grooves in the stone. One of these sections held the tintype of an extremely handsome young man, with dark hair worn long in the fashion of Lord Byron, and the pink cheeks always seen in tintypes. There was a hinged cover over it to protect it from the weather. From the legend cut in the stone below the picture, we learned that his name was Tristram Perkins. Tristram! Such a romantic name, we thought, just like a Knight of the Round Table!

The very oldest part of the cemetery sloped down almost to the river and there the stones were of slate, carved with the weeping willows and the lugubrious epitaphs of the day. One of them interested me so much that I memorized it, and here it is:

> *Death early snatched me from the sweets of time,*
> *My spirit bore to yon celestial clime.*
> *Locked in the house of Death you too must lie.*
> *Prepare to meet thy God,*
> *Oh, learn to die.*

I felt sad to learn the other day that vandals have ransacked the cemetery, and have destroyed our stone picnic table. The tombstone of the handsome young Tristram is gone too, I hear. I wonder if the vandals, in a few crazy hours of destruction, got the pleasure we did from the sunny days we played at Cemetery Hill.

Goodwin's

Goodwin's! That's what we called it. There was only one Goodwin's, just as there's only one Macy's. Would you say "Macy's Department Store"? Certainly not. Nor would we say "Goodwin's Ice Cream Store". It occupied the space in Dock Square next to the old PO, which in turn was next to the river.

Remember how cool and shady Goodwin's was on a hot day, and how deliciously it smelled of chocolates? But the ice cream… that was the thing! There never <u>was</u> any ice cream like Goodwin's. And let's not have any indulgent smiles at an old lady's memories, for many a New Yorker has been heard to exclaim incredulously, "Why, it's better than Shrafft's!" And you know how New Yorkers are.

Roy Rand made this superlative ice cream right on the premises – often several times a day, the demand was so great. Into it went the richest, freshest cream, the sweetest, ripest strawberries from near-by fields, the most velvety chocolate, the rosiest peaches, the finest vanilla, coffee and ginger root. I know, because I've seen it made.

And on mornings when Frozen Pudding was to be served, Mina Goodwin could always be seen coming through Dock Square carrying a two-quart pitcher of whatever it was that gave frozen pudding its special flavor. Maine was a prohibition state, you know, and we weren't supposed to ask embarrassing questions. Whatever it was, I'm sure it was the best. As I've said, the ingredients were the finest obtainable, but it was Roy

Rand's skill which made this distinguished product what it was.

Today, when a child wants an ice cream, he goes just as he is, very likely in torn dungarees, dirty sweatshirt and filthy sneakers, to one of the innumerable places where it's sold. He orders a cone, pays for it from his wallet, and leaves, lapping as he goes.

How different it was sixty years ago! Getting an ice cream at Goodwin's was an event. You wouldn't dream of going in your play clothes. Your mother would see to it that you were properly washed, your hair combed and adorned with your perkiest hair ribbon (the bigger the bow, the better). Then you would put on a starchy, freshly laundered dress and your best shoes, and sally forth clutching your dime. No wallets then. There were no cones in those days, so getting an ice cream meant sitting up like a lady at one of the round tables in the cool 'parlor'.

When you arrived, you'd try and get a table by the big window looking out on the piazza, where the Summer People congregated, and where you could see the sparkling blue river and watch the brightly colored canoes go by.

When the waitress arrived, you were faced with a weighty problem – what flavor should you choose? The waitress was usually patient while you deliberated, and at last the choice was made. Mine was usually ginger and chocolate.

At last the great treat arrived. You took very small spoonsful so as to make the ice cream, with all its velvety richness, last as long as possible. You all but lapped your saucer to get every last bit, but all too soon it was gone and you rose reluctantly. "Come straight home," your mother had said. And you did.

Just as you left, the trolley car, with a great jangling of bells, stopped in the Square. "Kennebunkport! End of the line," shouted the conductor.

Kennebunkport Recollections

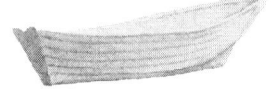

Winter

Perhaps you are thinking that we hibernated during the long, cold winter in Kennebunkport. No, indeed! To be sure we didn't have modern luxuries but what we'd never had we didn't miss. We heated our houses and did our cooking with coal or wood stoves. Few houses had indoor plumbing, though most people did have pumps in their sinks.

The period I speak of was the first few years of the twentieth century, and to all intents and purposes we were still in the nineteenth. Central heating, gas and electricity were common in the cities, but they had not as yet penetrated to the villages. After 1905 the modern world came with a rush, and I think it is a wonderful thing to have seen it develop – to have seen the country change almost overnight from a world not too different from pioneer days (a world of stoves, kerosene lamps, outhouses, washings done and baths taken in galvanized tubs, and all our vehicles horse-drawn), with practically no machinery, to our present mechanized civilization.

But of course we children didn't give a thought to all that. In spite of the cold we played out of doors almost as much as in summer, for we were warmly clothed. Boys and girls alike wore heavy fleece-lined, long-legged, long-sleeved and high-necked undergarments. We girls wore woolen petticoats under our cotton ones and woolen dresses over that. We wore long, black stockings too, and some of us had gaiters, made of very heavy, fleece-lined black jersey, which buttoned with an endless number of buttons above the knee. Of course we all wore high black laced or buttoned shoes. The boys' shoes fastened like ski boots with hooks. But we didn't have overshoes or snow boots, just rubber slip-ons. I must say it took forever to get into all these layers of clothing, but when the task was accomplished we could withstand almost anything in the way of weather. And this was a good thing, because there were no school busses and no days out for bad weather.

Then as now, sledding and skating were the principal sports but with a difference. Boys' sleds were low so they could go down hills belly-bumper. Girls' sleds were higher, and often elaborately decorated. I had one painted dark green, and decorated with two large roses, one red and one yellow, and for a special touch my name in large gold letters. I was so proud of that sled! Mr Perkins, who had a paint store over the river, painted it. I shouldn't be surprised if he would have become an artist if he were living today. Flexible Flyers came in a little later.

When I look at today's shoe-skates I marvel that we could skate at all. I wonder how we kept our skates on in those days. There was a heel strap and a toe strap for girls and they went right over our regular shoes. There were clamps for the boys, since their shoes were heavier. If we girls pulled the straps tight enough to hold the skates steady, it cut off the circulation, and soon our feet would be numb. Oh well, when they got numb enough we no longer felt the cold!

Of course, there were no skating rinks, but where the Catholic church now stands was a meadow which always flooded and then froze. It was a wonderful place to skate, with no danger of drowning when the ice was thin.

But the best place was the mill pond. Mr James Perkins who owned the grist mill, now converted into a restaurant by his grandson, would sometimes close the gates which held the tide water back, and in a few frigid nights the surface would be hard and glassy. Of course we children would visit it several times daily until the cry went out, "The ice is safe!" and how we would hurry home for our skates!

But it wasn't the children only who enjoyed this sport. On nights when the moon was full, the whole town would be out. There was one old man who had a pair of wooden skates, and he could cut circles around most of us – and did, literally. We gazed at him with awe.

There was always a big bonfire on the ice close to the shore, where we could warm our numb fingers and toes, and watch the older boys and girls skylarking[6]. They weren't segregated then into a separate part of society called teenagers. They were just boys and girls, and it seems to me they were happier. We didn't know there was such a thing as adolescence, and a good thing too! Our parents made no effort to understand us, so far as I can remember. They gave us love and discipline, and weren't always analyzing us and themselves. If we didn't turn out well they could always say, "He's just like Grandfather Bixby."

---

[6] Skylarking – Pass time by playing tricks or practical jokes; indulge in horseplay

Kennebunkport Recollections

Pungin'

Ever go pungin'? Unless you're sixty-ish you probably don't even know what a pung is, let alone what an exciting sport pungin' could be in the winter when the snow was on the ground.

I'll explain first that a pung was like a small horse-driven pickup truck on runners, and was used for the same purposes. Farmers used them to bring produce to market and to carry home bags of grain and other necessities, and store owners used them to deliver orders.

But we children used them for rides. When the owner wasn't looking we would slip our sled ropes around one of the runners and away we would go, sometimes with a regular whiplash effect if the horse, bored with standing, started up suddenly.

This sport could be exciting and even dangerous, for the roads were often deeply rutted or icy or both, and sometimes a driver who happened to be in a disagreeable mood would drive very fast in an attempt to shake us off. Of course we could let go of the sled rope (if things got really rough) but usually it was a matter of pride to hang on.

But pungs (or sleighs – in fact some children didn't say pungin', but teamin' – catching on teams) weren't our only means of getting a free ride. The best were the great, two-horse sleds which carried the heavy loads like logs, and big cakes of ice for the icehouses. These required a different technique. We stood on the runners, which were several inches wide and projected a foot or so beyond the main body of the sled. So they offered a safe, comfortable footing and we could steady ourselves by holding onto the poles which kept the loads from falling off.

I remember one February day in particular. There had been a big snowstorm a day or so before but Saturday morning dawned clear and windless. We children were all out early, for the big sleds were filling the hotel icehouses down at the Point and we could ride all day long. The air was sharp and clear, all a-glitter with sunlight on fresh snow and a-jingle with sleigh bells and the cloudless sky arching overhead. The sky was so blue you couldn't believe it.

As we rode along Ocean Avenue, the river was visible only in the deep channel and sparkled blue-green in the sunlight. Sometimes a fishing boat, its sail white against the blue of the water, would make its way down the channel to the ocean just beyond. Of course, the big sleds with their heavy loads didn't move very fast so there wasn't much excitement. But somehow it gave us a feeling of being "monarchs of all we surveyed" as we moved slowly along in stately fashion, watching the smaller vehicles which passed us and chatting with whatever friend occupied the other runner.

All day long we rode back and forth, pausing only a half hour or so at noon for dinner. (Yes dinner, not lunch!) We would go down on the loaded sleds, and I remember how the great blocks of ice looked – glittering crystal clear in the sunlight but a pale green in their depths. At the hotel icehouses, an empty sled would usually be pulling away as we drove up, and back to the village we would go, never tiring.

But that night we nodded at the supper table and soon after needed no urging to get into our flannel nightgowns and jump into our deep feather-beds already warmed by hot bricks or soapstones or flatirons, placed there by mothers who knew how it would be with us after a long day in the open air.

That was a long time ago, in another world.

Kennebunkport Recollections

The Day I Quit Writing for Good

When I was barely thirteen, I had an experience which soured me on writing for a good many years. I was a freshman in high school, and I had arrived there with a thorough training in grammar but absolutely no experience in composition. In those days there was no fooling around with discussion or motivation. Get right down to business, that was the idea. So, as we were packing our books after our first English class Miss Crowley, our pretty young teacher, said casually, "Tomorrow, bring in a theme describing your favorite room." That's easy, I thought, and wrote most of it in study hall. It never occurred to me to do otherwise than to follow her directions literally!

The next morning I went cheerfully to school, conscience clear, homework done. English was our first class, and I took my theme from my notebook, ready to pass in. Then the blow fell.

"You will read your themes aloud," said Miss Crowley, "beginning with the As."

To a shy and self-conscious child this was bad enough, but as the readings progressed I realized miserably that my theme was all wrong. It was plain that my classmates from other schools were accustomed to composition, and they rhapsodized about harmonizing colors and views from the windows until I thought I couldn't bear it any longer. Then it was my turn. With scarlet face and pounding heart I rose and delivered my opus, which ran something like this:

"Our living room is thirty feet long and twenty feet wide. In the middle of the outside wall there is a fireplace. On each side of the fireplace there is a bookcase, and at one end of each bookcase there is a window seat, and over each window seat there is a large window…" and so on. After what seemed eons I finished, and sat down.

"Well, Miss Hanson," said the teacher drily, "that makes me think of the riddle, 'once there was a green hill, and on the green hill there was a green house, and in the green house there was a white house, and in the white house there was a red house, and in the red house were some little black babies'." The class roared.

One after another the other children rose and read their themes but I didn't hear them. I was too absorbed in my own humiliation. At last the bell rang and the class was over. Finally, too, the endless day did end and I hurried home to cry my eyes out in the safe shelter of my room.

However, I knew now what the teacher wanted, and I proceeded to supply it. Soon I was asked to write for the school paper, but I refused. Me write? Ridiculous!

The Olympian Club

When I look at the Olympian Club today, I can hardly believe its humble beginnings! I don't remember the exact date, but I'd say about 1904. My Mother, my cousin Bertha Sherman (then Bertha Smith) and their friends started it. They were all bent on culture – and how they studied!

First it was literature. They began with mythology, and studied English authors from Beowulf right up through the Victorian poets. Then, having wrung all the juice from literature, they started on Nature. They studied birds, wild flowers, ferns, trees, mosses, even seaweeds.

They were considered a bit odd at the time. All that study! Better be attending to their homes and families. Remember, this was when education for women was considered a foolish waste of time and money. Bertha had graduated from Mt Holyoke when it was a two-year college, but that was considered locally as a peculiar thing to do. It was said that she cooked with a book open on the kitchen table. Well, she did – and I admit her cooking showed it. But she was one of the most interesting conversationalists I ever met.

But the club didn't study all the time. In the winter they had parties, and in the summer there were clambakes. I always went to them because baby-sitters were unheard of in those days. I remember one party at Carrie Colman's (then Carrie Wells). Each couple was provided with tall cooks' hats and a recipe, and the ingredients were set forth around the kitchen. The results were terrific!

And the clambakes! They were really something. A couple of husbands would go early to make the round stone pit which would hold the food, and build a fire inside it which would heat the stones to cook it. A couple of hours later the rest of the party would arrive, laden with all the ingredients of a really super bake, as well as homemade doughnuts and the club coffee pot. Sometimes clams were dug on the spot and cunners[7] caught from the rocks. Seaweed in large quantities had to be collected, and when the stones of the pit were hot enough, in went the clams in burlap bags, lobsters, cunners wrapped in corn husks, potatoes, eggs wrapped in scraps of newspaper, and plenty of corn. All this was alternated with layers of seaweed, and the whole covered with more seaweed.

Once finished, there was time for the grownups to stroll on the beach, while we children waded in the tide pools, collected crabs and sea-urchins, interesting stones or pretty shells. We also liked to climb among the rocks and jump from ledge to ledge.

When the bake was nearly ready, the children collected driftwood for a second fire, and the huge old gray enamel club coffee pot was brought forth. The grounds were mixed with eggs, the water added, and soon the most delectable fragrance in the world would arise.

At last the bake was done, and so was the coffee. Every woman had provided tin plates enough for her

---

[7] Cunners – A small fish (Tautogolabrus adspersus) common along the shore of the eastern United States. It is edible and its musky taste is considered a delicacy by some.

family – no paper plates then - and every plate was piled high. How we ate! No diets in those days. We'd eat until we could no longer move, but just sat there supremely content, watching the gulls and smelling the salt air.

Of course there are always people whose capacity is limitless, and if pressed would agree to eat just one more doughnut. And no wonder! We had some marvelous cooks in the Olympian Club, and not one would have dreamed of bringing doughnuts that had soaked the least bit of fat. Most women used sour milk if they had it, and the resulting nutty flavor and springy texture were something to remember.

At last the picnickers would summon enough energy to clean up the debris and drift off by families, until only the gulls were left. Ah, those were the days!

Riding the Electrics

"Town House! Change for Kennebunkport and Cape Porpoise! This car for Kennebunk, West Kennebunk, Sanford, Wells, Agunquit and York Beach, Kettery, Portsmouth and Dover!" In the first quarter of the century this cry was familiar to every man, woman and child in the seacoast area, for that's the way we got around in those days, before cars were within the reach of practically everyone. We didn't miss what we'd never had, and we thought the 'electrics' were one of the wonders of modern science. They went everywhere the trains didn't, and some of them were positively luxurious! One really deluxe model ran from Portland to Lewiston, and there was one on the Biddeford line that was pretty special, we thought. It had large, comfortable seats upholstered in purple plush and the woodwork was fancy indeed.

In the winter these conveyances were strictly utilitarian, but ah the summer – when the open cars were put on! There were two positions that brought joy to the hearts of the children – any end seat was good, but the front seat, just behind the motor man, was perfect. No convertible ever brought more joy, especially on a summer day when the wind of our swift passage cooled our hot faces and blue through our thin clothing.

Sometimes on Sunday afternoons we'd travel through the woods to the Cape Porpoise Casino, which has long since burned down but which once stood on the ledge near the wharf. It was a delightful place, with a wide shaded piazza facing the sea and a beautiful floor for dancing. You could get a fine shore dinner there, too. It was cool there on the hottest days. The grownups liked to sit in the rocking chairs on the piazza and watch the boats come and go in the harbor, but we children preferred to race up and down the ledges and slide on the polished dance floor, or go down to the wharf and watch the fishing boats come in.

Another favorite excursion place was the Nubble Light, a pleasingly long and varied ride from Kennebunkport. Sometimes the cars traveled through the woods and the trees came right to the tracks; so, from the vantage point of the end or front seat, we could look directly into the forest and see birds and small animals or an occasional deer, going about their daily business. Of course we passed through towns too, and as the electrics didn't go very fast we had plenty of chances to observe what went on there.

The Atlantic Shore Line (ASLR) went to Sanford also, and then as today women liked to visit the Goodall Mills for woolens. Along the way were little shelters where people waiting for the trolleys could sit, and one – Number 10 – was of special interest to me, for it was the station nearest my grandfather's farm and we often alighted there to be met by some member of the family with a horse and buggy in the summer or a sleigh in the winter.

In those days much of our shopping was done in Biddeford or Portland and of course we went on the electrics. As I remember, the fare from the junction to Biddeford was twenty cents. In the winter good theatrical companies came to Biddeford and Portland, and Kennebunkporters, rich with dollars extracted from the

Summer People, often took advantage of this entertainment.

Once a year most children had a terrific spree at Old Orchard, which was easily reached by trolleys connecting with the ASLR at Biddeford. As do children today, we rode on everything, ate indigestible messes, and enjoyed ourselves thoroughly.

Strange how quickly the trolley car era passed. I suppose today's buses fill the same place in people's lives. Perhaps modern children get the same thrill from travelling in an air-conditioned bus that we did from riding on the front seat of an open trolley car. But I doubt it!

Kennebunkport Recollections

Barkers Ridge

Take Route 1 until you come to Centerville, then turn left on a dirt road. Go almost straight up for a mile and you'll find yourself on Barker's Ridge. The road along the ridge is narrow and deeply rutted. In summer blinding dust clouds rise from it. In Spring and Fall the mud is ankle-deep, except on cold nights when the ruts freeze iron-hard and walking is a hazardous business. The people who live on Barker's Ridge develop an odd kind of shuffling gait from walking over these frozen ruts in the dark, feeling with their feet for obstacles in their path. In winter the wind from the mountains packs the snow in solidly, and only the stone walls which border the road on either side remain to mark its position. Sometimes for weeks during the stormy season the children run like squirrels along these walls to school.

Eventually the men, prodded by their long-suffering wives, will pry themselves loose from the cider barrel and radio long enough to plough the road to town, perhaps even around the circle. But this takes time, what with stops with convivial neighbors along the way.

The houses along Barker's Ridge are mostly tar paper "camps" with an occasional weather-beaten farmhouse. Almost everyone has a car, and everyone has a radio, but there the luxuries cease – unless you count children as luxuries. On Barker's Ridge they're a necessary evil.

About half-way to the place where the road seems to end live the Warners, Albert and Emma with their fifteen children. Their house has paint on it and they have a bathroom. Emma has been on the school board for a dozen years, and the job of school janitor is hereditary in the Warner family. The back seat in the left-hand corner of the schoolroom belongs by fiercely-defended right to the oldest Warner then in school, and woe betide the teacher who tries to dislodge him!

Albert and Emma are a devoted couple but fiercely jealous, and there is a young woman "down the road a piece" whom Emma at one time suspected of making advances to Albert, and the affair came to a head in an epic battle in the schoolhouse yard just after the Christmas program. Albert tried to separate the enraged women, but was soundly kicked, bitten and scratched for his pains. Albert, on his side, refuses to claim one of the sons as his, because he was born after Emma had been having a "wild spell."

Just across the road from Warner's is a tar paper shack where the oldest Warner boy, Eddie, lives with his wife Lillie and their three children. Lillie is only twenty and likes to "go", and Eddie lost his license some time ago for drunken driving; so what is more natural than that Eddie's brother Walter should take her to all the dances, while Eddie minds the children! Eddie thinks it's awful nice of Walt to take her. One night though, they stayed out a bit too late and Lillie found the door locked. This she considered uncalled for. So she seized a rock from the door yard and "hove" it through the glass part of the door. Eddie didn't put in a new glass until Spring, and it was a cold winter.

Go along the Ridge a little farther and you'll come to the Whitcomb place, where I boarded during my three years as teacher at the Barker's Ridge school. A big, black two-story house it was – black outside from years of weathering, and black inside from the smoke of countless fires. There was a pane of glass out of one of the "settin' room" windows, and the gap was filled with an old shirt. But marvelous meals came from the old black range in the kitchen – snowy, feather-light rolls, and mashed potatoes in a fluffy mound on an old cracked platter. There'd be a huge lump of home-made butter on top making golden rivulets down the sides as it melted, and a wreath of spicy home-made sausages around it. Mrs Whitcomb cured her own hams too, in the brick oven, and there she baked the Saturday night beans and Indian pudding.

After supper she'd put several kerosene lamps on the center table in the sitting room and we'd draw our rocking chairs up to the stove, full of good big oak sticks. On the table there's be a bowl of huge, red Macs, and very likely another of popcorn dripping with butter. Sometimes some of the neighbors would drop in and we'd play Flinch, or listen to hill-billy records on the little phonograph.

One day in March there was a blocking snowstorm and school was closed. But overhead the day was gorgeous. The sap was running in the sugar orchard, so I put on my snowshoes and went down the hill to help. All day we gathered sap, tended the fire in the brick-lined trench called the arch, and stirred the boiling sap in the big black pans. I shall always remember that day – the deep, cloudless blue of the sky, the sparking white of the fresh snow, the dark, lowering pines and the gray old maples.

The Whitcombs were God-fearing people, but "down under the mountain" lived the Maynards and they were indeed cats of another color. The patriarch of the family was old Saul – far and wide called the Chieftain, and well he merited the name for he could "take down" any of his boys if they foolishly ventured to oppose him. By local standards he was "well-fixed" but he never bought a car. Instead he drove an immense high old market wagon on which he rode aloft, looking down on lesser beings.

His youngest son was the apple of his eye, but he never gave him a name because, as he said, he wanted him to choose his own when he was grown. So on the school register the boy's name was Handy Andy, but his father always referred to him as "my little mannie" and the other children called him Mannie.

Physically, he was a beautiful child with curly blond hair, white rose-flushed skin, sparkling blue eyes, and a sturdy well-formed body. His manners, when he chose, were almost polished. But he had a sadistic strain. Children and small animals were afraid of him.

One important source of the Chieftain's income was a cider mill where, when work was slack, most of the Ridge men spent their days and quite often their nights too. The Chieftain's wife, who had died giving birth to Mannie her 16th child, had been a pretty, dainty woman who often had to get a meal stepping over the bodies of her husband's customers. Ridge women didn't complain of their husbands' absence as much as you might have expected because, as one of them explained to me, it gave them a better chance of escaping an annual pregnancy.

Had it not been for my friend Lucinda, my stay on Barker's Ridge would have been even drearier than it was. She lives in a one-story farmhouse down the lane from Warner's. The house is black outside from lack of paint, but bright and cheerful within, and always full of children and dogs, sunshine and laughter. There are plants in every window, plants like Lucinda – big and bright and strong. She is nearly six feet tall, with curly auburn hair, bright brown eyes which never miss anything, and the face of a merry child. She weighs over three hundred pounds, but she is quick as a cat on her feet, and as light. No one is in greater demand as a partner at the local dances, to which she always takes all four of her children, for she can't bear to think of their missing any fun.

Her husband Elmer is a tall, silent man who loves his wife and children dearly, but prefers to stay at home evenings with his pipe and his paper, though he will take an occasional hand at Sixty-three[8] when the neighbors drop in, which they do nearly every night in winter. Then, with dishes full of big, juicy apples and the dishpan heaped with popcorn, yellow with melted butter, the radio going full blast and ten or fifteen people of all ages, each trying to make himself heard above the racket, Lucinda's house is a merry place indeed. But there is never any hard cider around. Lucinda doesn't hold with drinking.

Barker's Ridge people love their school, and take considerable pride in its appearance. Every summer it is thoroughly cleaned, and papered and painted if necessary. And that's more than can be said of many rural neighborhoods whose over-all standards are considered a good bit higher than those of the Ridge.

---

[8] Sixty-three – a card game

People love to drop in occasionally, and point to the seats where they used to sit and to their initials carved here and there about the building – their 'footprints on the sands of time' I suppose.

Once a year at Christmas time the people of Barker's Ridge forget their feuds, which are many and bitter, and come to the schoolhouse for the Christmas program. For weeks the children have been practicing for the entertainment. All the rest of the year they had remained stubbornly silent when music was attempted, but now it developed that they could sing like birds! They willingly remained after school to practice, and to make wreaths and ropes of evergreen for decoration.

One of the Warner boys got the tree of course. His mother is on the school board, isn't she? Always has been, so far as any of the children can remember. So of course he gets the tree. It's a huge one, too – a point of pride. Everyone brings decorations from home, and besides these there are the paper chains and bells the smaller children have been making for weeks. The little Lothrop boy brings a big, shining star for the very top. The Star of Bethlehem on Barker's Ridge!

Seven o'clock and the guests begin to arrive. The head of each family brings a lantern, which is hung from one of the many hooks on the ceiling. The box stove is full of oak chunks and the room is hot. Soon the air reeks with the mingled fumes of kerosene, fir boughs, cheap perfume, winter underwear, stale tobacco and the Chieftain's cider. But no one is drunk that night. Barker's Ridge etiquette forbids it.

The program begins. The children sing and recite their 'pieces' to loud applause and stamping. Then comes the tree, and not a soul in the room is forgotten. Poor old Jake Sims, who isn't too bright, weeps into his little tarlatan bag of popcorn and candy. One of the Maynard boys, just bailed out of jail by the Chieftain, sits in a corner softly playing carols on his harmonica. There is much horseplay among the older boys and girls, but nothing really rough. The men gather in one corner discussing prospects of a hard winter while the women, like women everywhere, speak of recipes and children.

At the end of the evening, fathers buttoned their heavy coats and took their lanterns down from the hooks. Mothers hustled small children, fretful and sleepy, into their wraps. Young people paired off for the ride home with much giggling on the part of the girls and loud and pointed remarks from the young men. Cars started up in the yard, with a great churning of engines.

As I stood near the door bidding the guests good night, a sharp scream split the air, followed instantly by a slap like the crack of a pistol shot. Emma Warner and her rival, forced by public opinion to restrain their antagonism during the exercises, had reached the breaking point simultaneously and the battle was on.

Had the men who tried to separate them been familiar with Kipling's remarks concerning the female of the species, they would doubtless have agreed whole-heartedly, for they soon retired from the fray to nurse their wounds and wait for the best woman to win. But nobody won. As suddenly as it had begun the fight was over, and the participants were hustled into the waiting cars by their respective husbands. And everyone drove away.

I went to the school house again to see if the fire was safe to leave, and a glint of light from the tree caught my eye. The Star still shone on Barker's Ridge.

The Street Where I Live

Turn right off Charles Street, at a big yellow house with white blinds, and there you are on Broad Street, the street where I live. Broad Street is not like any other street in the little New Hampshire city of which it is a part. Indeed, it doesn't seem to be a part, but is more like a small community all by itself, separate. And it is separate. On one side thick green woods of pine and hemlock cut it off from the rest of the town, and on the other the river runs in a deep ravine. The woods give it the look of a summer resort and you half expect to see a lake glinting through the trees.

Broad Street ends in a pine grove. Great tall giants they are, and from them the ground slopes sharply to the intervale, and beyond that flows the river.

The intervale is a joy in summer. Little paths crisscross it, leading who knows where, and along the paths grow blueberries and wild strawberries. Raccoons live there and sometimes a colony of beavers will cut a few trees along the river bank to build a dam. As I said, Broad Street is different.

Broad Street is a pleasant street. Maples border it on both sides, for deep shade in summer and a golden glory in the fall. In the spring their red buds lift the heart after the long, dark northern winter.

The houses on Broad Street are all different, and we like it that way. Some are imposing red brick structures in the Georgian manner; some are in the tasteless but comfortable style of the early 1900s; and one, my own small cottage, has the steep-roofed look of a fisherman's house by the harbor in some Maine seacoast village. But every house has a large and well-kept lawn and a wealth of gay flowers in summer. The houses are kept well painted too. Broad Street people take great pride in their homes.

The sidewalks on Broad Street are different. From the generally prosperous look of the houses, you would expect to see trim cement walks on both sides of the street, but that's not the way it is. One side of the street has them, but the other side most people prefer to let their lawns run right down to the pavement. It's pleasant walking on the thick, soft grass under the maples in summer.

Broad Street is a friendly place. There are no fences, and the neighbors wander at will through one another's back yards with plants or spicy cookies fresh from the oven to share, or perhaps just to have a chat with whoever happens to be outside gardening, or just enjoying the day.

Snow on Broad Street

Snow! It seemed as if I couldn't bear it another minute!

Early in December was when it had started and there had been no let-up, no welcome break in the cold, so that we could get a glimpse of bare ground before winter by the calendar really set in. Christmas week brought a blizzard, and from then on storm followed storm with never a thaw, and the banks along the streets grew higher and higher, until each house seemed isolated from its neighbors, no matter how close. With each succeeding storm the street grew narrower, because there was less and less place to put the plowed-up snow. There was barely room for two cars to pass.

Now it was March, and for two days it snowed. The snow was waist-deep around my house and I could no longer reach the street or my garage. It was useless to have the paths and the driveway shoveled before the storm was over and the street could be plowed. I was alone, cut off from my friends and my daily activities, trifling though they were.

I thought of starting my Spring cleaning, or painting woodwork and floors, of telephoning friends. But I had not the energy. I felt as if every flake were resting right on me, weighing me down.

But after two days the storm did stop, the street plow came, my neighbor boy shoveled the paths and the driveway, and I was free! The sun came out and the warm winds blew. The city trucks came and began to cart away the snow and opened the drains.

Spring, long despaired of, was really on the way!

Progress

One of the many interesting things about being 75 is to have seen this whole modern world come. I suppose the middle-aged today like to tell their children about the time when there was no television, only radio, and I suppose today's children will tell <u>their</u> children about the thrill of seeing the first man on the moon. Goodness knows what *their* children will look back upon!

One big difference I can see as I look back upon my childhood days is the slow spread of change. Then in 1895 until 1900, it all came in a rush. When I was born in Dorchester, Massachusetts, we lived in an apartment with a bathroom, gas and electricity. But four years later when we came to Kennebunkport, the only indoor plumbing in town, to my knowledge, was in the places which catered for the Summer People. Gas was unknown, but there was electricity in the hotels and summer boarding houses. And there are still isolated spots where people are living much as the pioneers did. I understand that many of the disillusioned youth of today who have grown up with every comfort have forsworn them all. I think that as they grow older, however, they'll be glad to come back to civilization.

The Depression made a big change in the country's lifestyle. Even rich people, whose dividends were no longer forthcoming, could not afford to keep up their big summer "cottages" staffed by many servants, and spent their summers travelling or in Europe, where living was cheaper. The automobile had come into wide use by then and the roads were improving. So people were discovering America.

When the stock market rose again, they didn't come back to the big houses along the cliffs, but moved restlessly from place to place, as they still do. Now it's the working people who have cottages, usually at some lake, where they spend weekends and vacations.

Now there are no servants, except among the <u>very</u> rich. Negros don't care to be servants any longer, and immigrants go into the factories where they can earn more money and be independent.

Golf used to be a rich man's sport and the country club frequented only by society, but now there's a country club for almost any wage bracket.

For that was then, and this is now.

About Grace Brock

Elizabeth Grace Hill Hanson (known as Grace to friends and family) was born in 1895 to Gertrude Wilton (Hill) Hanson and Winfield E Hanson, in Dorchester Massachusetts. She had one brother, Richard (Dick) who was born in 1909.

Her father inherited some money from his father, and used it to train as a dentist. They then moved to Kennebunkport after he qualified, into a large and lovely home he designed himself. Grace remembered much about growing up here, later captured in a series of articles for the Star Press Inc.

After qualifying as a teacher, Grace worked for a time in Oklahoma, New York City, and Maine. She then married Leon Brock and had two daughters: Priscilla Mary in 1924 and Celia Elizabeth in 1927. Leon later left in 1930, and Grace brought up her daughters as a single mother on Broad Street in Rochester, New Hampshire, in a home her family bought for her. She supported the household through her work as a grammar school teacher.

Grace studied at summer school for her BA degree during those years, and in due course graduated (in 1946?) at the same ceremony as Priscilla. She went on to become a teacher of the 6th grade in Dover, and age group she enjoyed very much, and when she retired she received much praise for the outstanding work she had done with the students.

Grace aged 15 (right) with her parents
and young brother Dick (Richard)

Grace Hanson Brock